What in the World?

The Atomic Bomb

Jennifer Fandel

W W
What in the World?

Creative Education
an imprint of The Creative Company

Introduction

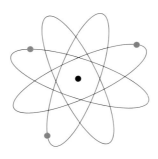

On July 16, 1945, a deafening explosion shattered the predawn silence of the New Mexican desert, and a light as bright as 20 suns filled the sky. Moments later, a giant cloud roiled in changing colors as it mushroomed into the atmosphere. The testing of the world's first atomic bomb filled J. Robert Oppenheimer and his team of scien-

An area of the New Mexican desert called Jornado del Muerto, or Journey of Death, was selected for the Trinity test site. Spanish explorers gave it this name because the scarcity of water made travel there perilous.

tists with mixed emotions. From the splitting of atoms, they had generated an unprecedented amount of power. Accompanying this power was also the potential for unimaginable destruction. Within seconds of the explosion, the scientists realized that the world would never be the same again.

Nuclear weapons have been used only twice in the history of warfare, against Japan during World War II.

Despite his political leanings toward communism, Robert Oppenheimer was highly valued by the United States government.

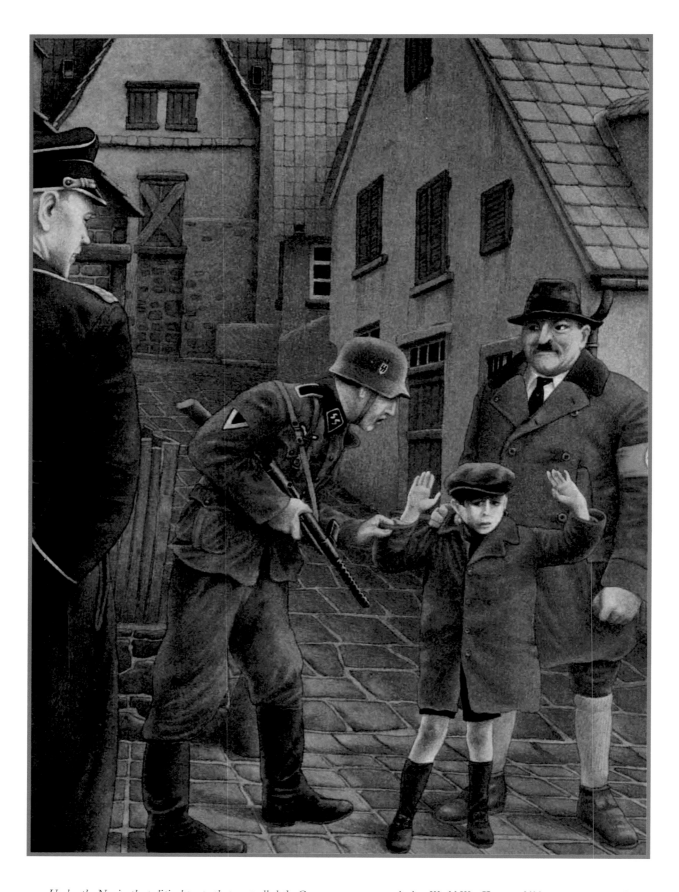

Under the Nazis, the political party that controlled the German government during World War II, even children were persecuted.

A World of Power

Between 1939 and 1945, when J. Robert Oppenheimer and his team were developing the atomic bomb, the world was rapidly fracturing into the black-and-white allegiances of World War II. No country was left untouched by the conflict's simple yet utterly disastrous cause: humanity's insatiable desire for power.

In Europe, German dictator Adolf Hitler invaded Poland in 1939, instigating the global conflict. Hitler blamed such people as Jews, Catholics, gypsies, and homosexuals for Germany's economic problems, and he had millions of those people—along with the elderly, ill, and disabled—transported to concentration camps, where many were systematically gassed to death. By the end of the war in 1945, approximately 9 million persecuted people, along with millions of soldiers and other combatants, had died throughout Europe.

German dictator Adolf Hitler was known for his stirring speeches and powers of persuasion.

The Lascaux caves were closed to the public in 1963 to preserve the paintings from further deterioration and damage.

The ruthless power of dictator Joseph Stalin also transformed the Soviet Union during this time. Stalin instituted massive industrialization and collectivized farming campaigns to make his country a living example of the successes of communism, a political system based on government control of property and enterprise. People in the Soviet Union had jobs, shelter, and food when the rest of the world was struggling through economic depression. But those outside the country didn't see the harsh dictatorship under which the people lived; anyone who disagreed with Stalin was liable to be killed, sent to a work camp in Siberia, or exiled from the country.

In 1940, schoolboys discovered the Lascaux caves in France. These cave walls contain paintings of horses, bison, and cattle completed around 14,000 to 13,500 B.C. by prehistoric peoples.

Russian artist Ivan Bilibin's fairy-tale subjects (opposite) helped people escape the reality of repression under Joseph Stalin.

Japan's ambitious desire for more land and power in Asia led to its invasion of China and Southeast Asia. Aligned with the Axis powers of Germany and Italy, Japan ignited the war in the Pacific with the bombing of the American naval base at Hawaii's Pearl Harbor on December 7, 1941. In preparation for an expected Allied invasion, the Japanese military created a kamikaze air force, suicidal pilots who crashed bomb-filled planes into their targets. In the spirit of the kamikaze, 28 million Japanese civilians were also trained to use primitive weapons, such as bamboo spears and pitchforks, against the enemy.

In the United States, women and African Americans found individual and collective power in their quest for equal treatment. Women, having won the right to vote in 1920, began entering the workforce in record numbers, especially once U.S. involvement in the war took men away from their jobs and into military positions. African American troops, who dealt with prejudice even within the military, began questioning why they were fighting for a country that did not treat them as equals. Their experiences would inspire many to push for civil rights in the following decades.

Many American women built weapons and planes (right)
to aid in the U.S.'s war against determined Japanese forces (opposite).

During World War II, the letter "V" appeared on walls in German-occupied Belgium, where it stood for *vriheid* (freedom) in Flemish and *victoire* (victory) in French. Soon, the letter appeared on walls throughout Europe.

French artist Marcel Duchamp's Nude Descending a Staircase, No. 2 *shows the influence of Cubism on early 20th-century art.*

Picasso's famous mural Guernica *was 11 1/2 feet (3.5 m) tall and almost 26 feet (8 m) wide.*

In 1937, Spanish artist Pablo Picasso painted *Guernica*, his masterpiece about the brutality of war, after fascist forces led by dictator Francisco Franco bombed the unsuspecting Spanish town of Guernica.

Likewise, challenging conventional ideas and finding new ways to portray the world was a mission that unified and empowered many artists in South America. Influenced by the European art movements of Cubism and Surrealism, South American painters—such as Chilean Roberto Matta and Peruvian José Sabogal—depicted the poverty and identity struggles of indigenous peoples in a time of intense political instability. The artists' recognition of these often-overlooked subjects helped them more clearly see—and champion—the richness and importance of their diverse cultures.

Curious George, *published in 1941, was followed by six more stories about the mischievous little monkey.*

German-born Albert Einstein and American Robert Oppenheimer were both brilliant physicists.

Curious George, a children's story about an inquisitive monkey, was published in 1941. The book's creators, H. A. and Margret Rey, fled Europe at the outbreak of the war to settle in New York.

However, developments by Europeans and Americans in the field of physics would alter the world most profoundly during this period. Physicist Albert Einstein, whose theory of relativity shattered commonsense notions of time and space being constant, also found that energy and mass were an interrelated part of this equation. This theory launched physicists on a pursuit to understand the atom—the most basic form of matter—and find a way to convert its mass to energy, something never before achieved. Drawn to this intellectual endeavor was J. Robert Oppenheimer, a man for whom mathematical formulas and imagination were entwined—and explosive.

A Calculated Life

J. Robert Oppenheimer was born in 1904 into a life of privilege, the elder son of a successful businessman father and artist mother. The family's spacious New York City apartment was filled with many original paintings by renowned artists, and servants kept their home spotless. A delicate dreamer and voracious reader who was prone to illness, Robert spent most of his time indoors, in a comfortable, though lonely, cocoon.

Robert's passion for science was ignited at age five, when his grandfather gave him a simple box of rocks. In the years that followed, he learned the scientific names of specific minerals and carefully labeled each new rock he found. When he was 12, Robert corresponded with well-known geologists about the minerals he found in New York's Central Park. Impressed by his observations, the New York Mineral Club invited him to deliver a lecture in 1916. Members were shocked to meet an awkward 12-year-old boy with disheveled hair.

In 1945, after the first atomic bombs were dropped, the desperate Japanese government asked schoolchildren to gather acorns to supplement the country's dwindling food supply. The acorns were then ground into flour.

Since his brother Frank was not born until Robert (pictured) was eight years old, Robert's sickly childhood was fairly solitary.

In 1945, three days after delivering the essential components of the atomic bomb to the U.S. military at the Pacific island of Tinian, the USS *Indianapolis* was torpedoed and sunk by the Japanese.

In 1953, the Soviet Union opened the world's first nuclear power station outside of Moscow. Since that time, severe nuclear accidents have happened at Three Mile Island in the U.S., in Chernobyl, Ukraine, and in Takaimura, Japan.

The Indianapolis *(opposite) sank within 12 minutes, taking 300 crewmen with it;*

the explosion of Chernobyl's main reactor in 1986 caused widespread contamination and death (above).

19

Oppenheimer's days as a brilliant student prepared him for a successful teaching career.

While the Oppenheimers's wealth kept Robert sheltered from many common difficulties, his schooling instilled in him a sense of responsibility to make the world a better place. Robert's Jewish family didn't attend synagogue but chose to attend lectures at the Ethical Culture Society instead. Robert also attended the society's school, excelling in its demanding environment. In addition to all the required courses—history, English literature, math, and physics—he added Greek, Latin, French, and German, earning straight As in every one.

In 1945, U.S. chemist Earl W. Tupper invented plastic bowls called Tupperware, which sealed without leaking. The containers, sold door-to-door and at home parties, were instantly popular.

Some women were so enthusiastic about the new Tupperware containers that they even fashioned hats out of the products.

Oppenheimer was invigorated and intrigued by the beautiful but harsh desert environment of the American Southwest.

In high school, Robert had only one friend, a boy named Francis Fergusson from New Mexico. After graduating in 1921, Robert fell ill on a trip to Germany, and his slow recovery kept him from attending Harvard University in the fall. However, in the spring, a trip to New Mexico to visit Francis restored his health and changed his outlook on life. Worlds away from the bustling city, the wild desert and quiet mountains freed him from his reclusive habits; he became more easy-going, spirited, and engaged in the world around him.

The vibrant New Mexican landscape also inspired the work (opposite) of famous American painter Georgia O'Keeffe.

Although Robert was bookish and unathletic, he loved to sail. His father bought him a sailboat when he was 16, and Robert became skilled at sailing through dangerous storms.

American artist Andy Warhol was known for using many popular subjects—such as Mickey Mouse—in his work.

When film producer Walt Disney showed a drawing of "Mortimer Mouse" to his wife Lillian in 1928, she quickly suggested renaming it "Mickey." Mickey became one of the most famous cartoon characters ever created.

Yet what New Mexico brought out in Robert, Harvard soon suppressed. Robert retreated into his studies and quickly discovered a passion for physics, which led him to pursue graduate work in 1926 at Germany's University of Göttingen. At that time, Göttingen was the center for theoretical physics, a new branch of the discipline that focused on the use of mathematical models instead of physical experiments to prove or disprove theories. Robert was awarded his doctoral degree at age 23, and he received job offers from some of the best universities in the world. Yet his fondness for New Mexico led him back to the American West.

Oppenheimer enjoyed reading with his children, Peter and Katherine (opposite), in the years after the bomb was used.

While nearly every building at ground zero in Hiroshima, Japan, was leveled by the bomb, the Trade Promotion Hall still stands. Renamed the A-Bomb Dome, it is a reminder of the atomic bomb's terrible power.

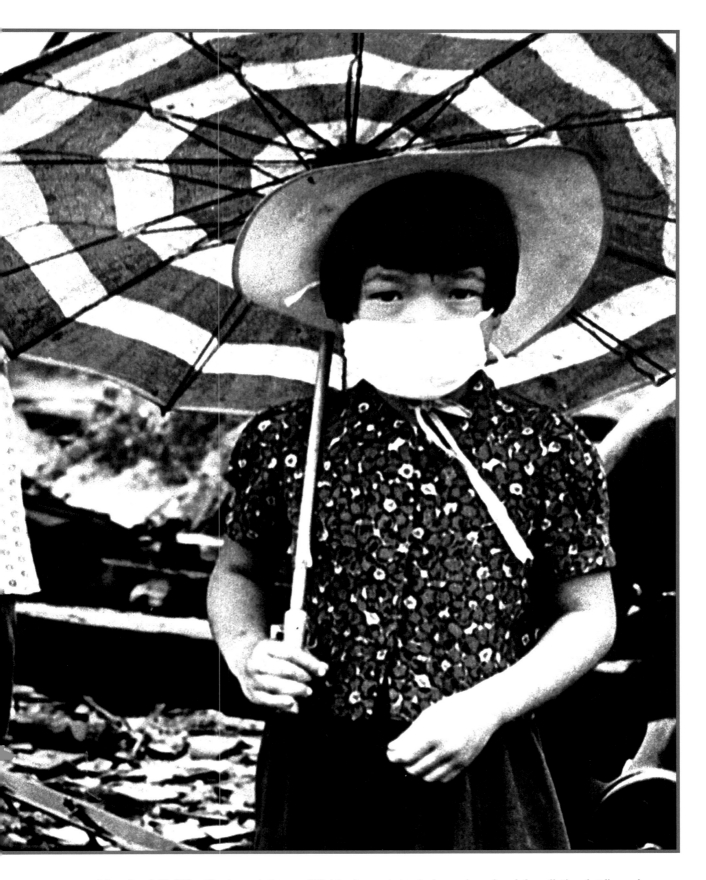

More than half of Hiroshima's population was killed by the atomic bomb; the survivors feared the radiation that lingered.

In the late 1920s and '30s, Robert split his time teaching and researching between the California Institute of Technology and the University of California at Berkeley, retreating to New Mexico's mountains to recover from the rigorous demands he made on himself. Although he seemed frail, his bright blue eyes reflected his mental stamina and the zeal he possessed for his work. At age 36, Robert married a 29-year-old botanist named Kitty Harrison. The couple would eventually have two children.

In 1939, war broke out in Europe, and the U.S. scientific community was stunned to learn that three scientists—Germans Otto Hahn and Fritz Strassmann, and Austrian Lise Meitner—had achieved the first nuclear fission, or splitting, of uranium atoms. Robert and his colleagues considered the ramifications: while nuclear fission could create a new energy source, it could also be used destructively—in a bomb. In this climate of fear and uncertainty, and under the direction of U.S. President Franklin Delano Roosevelt, Robert and scientists at 12 American universities began racing to beat the Germans to create the world's first atomic bomb.

Robert greatly underestimated the number of people and amount of money needed at Los Alamos. Only 100 people began the project, but 6,000 were working there by the end. The venture cost upwards of $2 billion.

Austrian physicist Lise Meitner (above); Oppenheimer and a group of American scientists (opposite).

In the summer of 1942, government officials placed Robert in charge of Berkeley's fast-neutron research to determine how much fissionable uranium would be necessary for an atomic bomb. Robert immediately organized a secret seminar of theoretical physicists, but knowledge alone would not be enough to see the project through. Not only would laboratories have to be built, but a uranium refining process would have to be developed, detonating explosives made more accurate, and everything down to the bomb's wiring be carefully planned. Time, from the moment the project began, was already ticking against them.

In the fall of 1942, Robert became director of the national bomb project, code-named the "Manhattan Project," and established headquarters in Los Alamos, New Mexico. Amidst the chaos of the immense project, Robert trained his mind on the atom—that which is too small to be seen with the human eye—and imagined a power large enough to transform the entire world.

The Flame of Peace burns at the Memorial Cenotaph in Hiroshima. A cenotaph honors those who have died, even though their remains lie elsewhere. Many victims of the atomic bombs were never found.

At Hiroshima's Peace Memorial Park, people can see the A-Bomb Dome and remember the horrific event it represents.

On December 7, 1941, when the Japanese attacked the U.S. naval base at Pearl Harbor, 2,043 Americans were killed.

In the early 20th century, war entered the global arena for the first time in history, and advances in science and technology took traditional warfare to new levels. Germ warfare and poisonous gases could extinguish an enemy without the risks of gun combat, and airplanes rained bombs on cities and towns, ravaging the land and killing innocent civilians. For every horror avoided, new ones were created. Fighting raged in Europe, Asia, Africa, and even touched North America with the bombing of Pearl Harbor during World War II. World leaders became desperate to find a way to end the enormous conflict.

When Adolf Hitler came to power in 1933, many Jewish scientists were fired from their positions. Robert and other scientists donated money to help them immigrate to the U.S.

Four days after Japan attacked Pearl Harbor, Germany and Italy, Japan's allies, also declared war on the U.S.

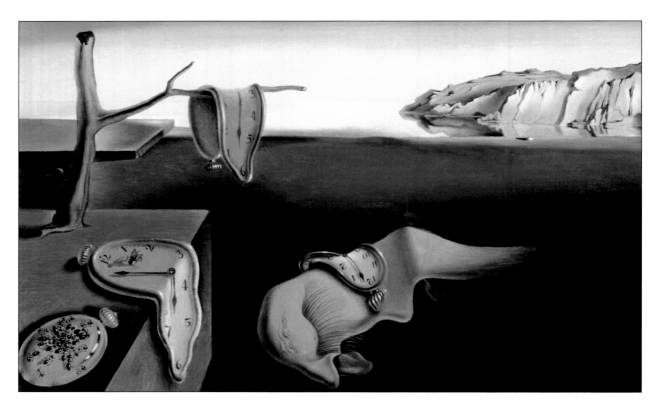

The Persistence of Memory, *by Spaniard Salvador Dali, is one of the most recognizable images of Surrealist art.*

Spanish artist Joan Miró's Group of Personages *shows his drastic opposition to traditional painting methods.*

America's famed Route 66 opened in 1926. The 2,448-mile (3,541 km) highway connected Chicago, Illinois, to Los Angeles, California, and was dubbed the "Main Street of America."

In the 1920s and '30s, the European Surrealist movement, which portrayed the world of dreams and imagination with illogical images—such as scenes of clocks melting and gigantic metronomes—spread its influence globally.

In only 28 months, from March 1943 to July 1945, Robert and his self-assembled team of scientists—including Hans Berthe, Edward Teller, and Edward Condon—built the world's first uranium and plutonium atomic bombs. The remote location and strict security measures at Los Alamos, which housed the weapons' research and design, kept the bombs hidden from prying eyes.

Before the project at Los Alamos began, Robert's scientific team at Berkeley had discovered how to create an uncontrolled chain reaction that would release nuclear energy in a massive explosion. In its normal state, an atom's nucleus is stable; its constant energy holds it together. In fission, however, when a fast-moving neutron strikes an atom's nucleus, the unstable nucleus splits into two nearly equal nuclei, which produce more neutrons to continue the process. To sustain that reaction, the scientists determined that they would need a large amount of fissionable uranium and plutonium.

After the interstate highway system was developed, portions of U.S. Route 66 were renamed "Historic Route 66."

35

In countries affected most by the war, every bit of food had to be carefully rationed.

For the uranium bomb, Robert's scientific team at Los Alamos found that a simple gun design would yield a powerful explosion, since a slug of fissionable uranium could be fired into a larger uranium target to begin the reaction. The plutonium bomb was more complex, though, because the fissionable plutonium couldn't be brought together fast enough to start a reaction. After months of experimenting, the scientists tried implosion. When detonated, explosives surrounding a sphere of plutonium would compress it, producing an explosion.

Argentina's rich agricultural lands helped feed much of Europe during World War II. After five years of exporting wheat and other crops, it became the richest country in South America.

In 1941, during the German siege of Leningrad in the Soviet Union, citizens had no heat or electricity and little food. People made soup out of boiled leather wallets and bread out of sawdust and seeds.

All across Europe, people were forced to abandon cities that were devastated by warfare and neglect.

The first self-sustaining nuclear chain reaction was achieved by physicists Enrico Fermi, Leo Szilard, and Edward Teller at the University of Chicago. All of these men would help build the first nuclear bombs.

In 1944, the Nazis found a brave Jewish family after they'd spent two years hiding in their home in Amsterdam, Holland. The world would learn their story through the diary of the daughter, Anne Frank.

Prior to the test of the plutonium bomb in July 1945, the climate at Los Alamos grew tense. Robert and his team knew this was the moment they had been working toward, and anything less than perfection was unacceptable. Too much time and money had been spent, and, although the war in Europe had come to an end, the conflict grew more violent in the Pacific each day. The scientists worked impossibly long hours in the desert heat, setting up hundreds of instruments, searchlights, and more than 50 cameras to record the explosion at a test site code-named "Trinity."

The 100-foot (30.5 m) tower from which the first atomic bomb was detonated (opposite); teenage diarist Anne Frank (above).

The explosion from the atomic bomb dropped on Nagasaki generated a 7,000 °F (3,871 °C) heat wave.

Named after the pilot's mother, the Enola Gay *became the property of the Smithsonian Institution in 1946.*

On July 12, the scientists assembled the plutonium core. Two days later, the core was taken to Trinity, and the bomb was hauled to the top of a 100-foot (30.5 m) tower. Late at night on July 15, the detonators were installed. The test would happen at 5:30 A.M. the next day.

In the final minutes of the countdown on July 16, Robert tried to steady himself. When the bomb ignited, Robert's drawn face relaxed, but the piercing light and numbing heat that accompanied the blast filled him with both amazement and fear. Into Robert's mind flashed a line from a sacred Hindu text, the *Bhagavad Gita*: "I am become Death, the shatterer of worlds."

After the test, scientists surveyed the extent of the explosion, measured as the equivalent of 20,000 tons (18,144 t) of TNT. The fireball had created a sloping crater in the earth and fused the desert sand into a greenish-gray glass. Every living thing—plants, snakes, squirrels, lizards, and even ants—within a one-mile (1.6 km) radius was destroyed.

Robert taught himself the ancient language of Sanskrit by reading the sacred Hindu book, *Bhagavad Gita*, Sanskrit for "The Lord's Song." Hindus believe that nothing is destroyed in the universe; instead, it is transformed in the circle of life.

After World War II, Robert was hailed as a hero in newspapers and magazines throughout the U.S. While he accepted the praise, he believed it was his duty to publicly raise his misgivings about the bomb.

Harry S. Truman led the U.S. at the end of the war.

The uranium bomb was originally nicknamed "Thin Man" after President Franklin Delano Roosevelt but was changed to "Little Boy" when the gun barrel detonator was shortened.

"Fat Man" was dropped by Major Charles Sweeney's bomber, Bockscar, *and detonated about 1,800 feet (550 m) above Nagasaki.*

"Fat Man," the pluto-nium bomb, was named after British Prime Minister Winston Churchill, a close ally of the U.S. Some thought the round bomb resem-bled the portly Churchill.

U.S. President Harry S. Truman was immediately notified of the bomb's success. With no clear end to the war in the Pacific in sight, Truman hoped using the atomic bombs would prompt Japan to finally surrender, saving many American lives. On August 6, 1945, American pilot Colonel Paul Tibbets Jr. flew his B-29 bomber, the *Enola Gay*, over Japan, dropping the uranium-core atomic bomb "Little Boy" on the city of Hiroshima. As Hiroshima's citizens were trav-eling to work and school, the 10-foot-long (3.1 m) and 9,000-pound (4 t) bomb exploded above the city, leveling it and killing 100,000 people. Three days later, the plutonium bomb "Fat Man" was dropped on Nagasaki, immediately killing 75,000. Survivors in both cities suffered radiation sickness, severe burns, and missing limbs. On August 14, Japan officially surrendered to Allied forces.

Allied leaders Winston Churchill, Franklin Roosevelt, and Joseph Stalin (left to right, opposite) in February 1945.

Robert initially believed that the atomic bomb—by threat alone—would eliminate the future of worldwide war. However, while he greatly underestimated the bomb's effects on the world at large, he never underestimated the human desire for power. Other countries immediately began making their own nuclear weapons—first atomic weapons, and then hydrogen fusion super bombs—competing with one another in a lethal "arms race."

More than 60 years later, the world's nuclear arsenal contains more than 20,000 nuclear weapons. In remote locations around the globe, within heavily fortified storage facilities, they sit. No dust is allowed to gather on them—whether large or small, of the dullest metal or the shiniest steel. They are ready for action, yet they continue to sit in stony silence. This is where their power lies. Whenever there is talk of war, their presence envelops the world like an ominous shroud.

In 1940, Africa's first national park, Serengeti National Park, was established in British-controlled East Africa. The park protected animals such as lions, giraffes, and rhinoceroses within its boundaries.

To produce the amounts of fissionable material needed to build the bombs, the U.S. government constructed factories in the remote towns of Oak Ridge, Tennessee, and Hanford, Washington.

APFICHES ATAR, GENÈVE

ATOMKRIEG NEIN

After the bombs were dropped, many people feared that nuclear war would erupt all over the world.

W
W
What in the World?

1904	J. Robert Oppenheimer is born in New York City.
1905	Albert Einstein publishes his theory of relativity, revolutionizing physics.
1908	The Hejaz Railway is completed in the Middle East, allowing travel from Damascus, Syria, to the holy city of Medina, Saudi Arabia.
1911	Norwegian explorer Roald Amundsen is the first person to reach the South Pole.
1914–1918	World War I is fought. Its brutality causes it to be called "the war to end all wars."
1915	The first long-distance telephone service begins, connecting the U.S. from coast to coast.
1920	Baseball's legendary slugger Babe Ruth begins his 14-year career with the New York Yankees.
1925	The Paris Exposition of Decorative Arts opens and influences the art deco movement in art and architecture.
1928	American Amelia Earhart becomes the first woman to fly across the Atlantic.
1931	Penicillin is used for the first time at the Royal Infirmary in Sheffield, England.
1933	Adolf Hitler becomes dictator of Germany. He begins World War II six years later by invading Poland.
1939–1945	World War II is fought, resulting in more than 54 million deaths worldwide.
1942	Oppenheimer accepts the position heading the Manhattan Project.
1945	On August 6 and 9, atomic bombs are dropped on Hiroshima and Nagasaki in Japan.
1949	British novelist George Orwell publishes *1984*, a novel illuminating life under a futuristic, totalitarian dictatorship.
1953	The U.S. tests the world's first nuclear-fusion device, the hydrogen bomb.
1957	Russia launches the satellite *Sputnik I*, sparking a "space race" with the U.S.
1964	The year's hit songs include "She Loves You" and "Love Me, Do" by the British group The Beatles.
1967	Oppenheimer dies of throat cancer at his Princeton, New Jersey, home.

The inspirational life and career of American pilot Amelia Earhart (opposite) continues to fascinate people today.

Copyright

Published by Creative Education
P.O. Box 227, Mankato, Minnesota 56002

Creative Education is an imprint of The Creative Company.
Design by Rita Marshall
Production design by The Design Lab

Photographs by Alamy (images-of-france, Michael Ventura), Corbis (Andy Warhol Foundation; The Barnes Foundation, Merion Station, Pennsylvania; Bettmann; Brooklyn Museum; Terry W. Eggers; Douglas Kirkland; Nagasaki Atomic Bomb Museum; Reuters; The State Russian Museum; John Van Hasselt), Getty Images (AFP, Archivo Iconografico, Hulton Archive, Keystone, Time Life Pictures), iStockphoto

Illustration copyright © 2007 Roberto Innocenti (6), © 2007 Mark Summers (39, 46), © 1954 Hans Erni (cover, 45)

Cover illustration by Hans Erni

Library of Congress Cataloging-in-Publication Data
Fandel, Jennifer.
The atomic bomb / by Jennifer Fandel.
p. cm. — (What in the world?)
Includes index.
ISBN-13: 978-1-58341-555-9
1. Atomic Bomb—History. 2. Oppenheimer, J. Robert, 1904-1967.
3. Nuclear physicists—United States—Biography. I. Title. II. Series.

UG1282.A8F35 2007   623.4'5119—dc22   2006027449

First Edition
9 8 7 6 5 4 3 2 1

Index